THE GREAT OUTDOORS

Freshwater Fishing

By Ellen Hopkins

Consultant:
Anne Glick
Director of Education
American Sportfishing Association

CAPSTONE
HIGH-INTEREST
BOOKS

an imprint of Capstone Press
Mankato, Minnesota

Capstone High-Interest Books are published by Capstone Press
151 Good Counsel Drive, P.O. Box 669, Mankato, Minnesota 56002
http://www.capstone-press.com

Library of Congress Cataloging-in-Publication Data
Hopkins, Ellen.
    Freshwater fishing/by Ellen Hopkins.
    p. cm.—(The great outdoors)
    Includes bibliographical references and an index (p. 48).
    ISBN 0-7368-0915-5
    1. Fishing—Juvenile literature. [1. Fishing.] I. Title. II. Series.
SH445 .H67 2002
799.1'1—dc21   00-012553

Summary: Describes the equipment, skills, conservation issues, and safety concerns of
freshwater fishing.

Editorial Credits
Carrie Braulick, editor; Lois Wallentine, product planning editor; Timothy Halldin,
    cover designer and illustrator; Katy Kudela, photo researcher

Photo Credits
Brian Parker/TOM STACK & ASSOCIATES, 42 (bottom)
Capstone Press/Gary Sundermeyer, cover (bottom left, bottom right), 4, 9 (foreground),
10, 13, 14, 17, 18 (foreground), 21, 22, 26, 28–29, 36
Comstock, Inc., 1, 9 (background), 18 (background)
Jeff Henry/Roche Jaune Pictures, Inc., 6, 39
Kent and Donna Dannen, 44
Kim Halldin/Halldin Graphic Design, cover (top right)
Photo Network/Jim Schwabel, 34
Photri-Microstock, 40 (top)
Rob and Ann Simpson, 41 (top)
Unicorn Stock Photos/Aneal Vohra, 32
Visuals Unlimited/Patrice Ceisel, 40 (bottom), Steve Maslowski, 41 (bottom),
    Wally Eberhart, 42 (top)
William H. Mullins, 30

Table of Contents

CHAPTER 1

Freshwater Fishing

People have been freshwater fishing for thousands of years. It is one of North America's most popular sports. North America offers many freshwater streams, rivers, and lakes for people to enjoy the sport.

History of Fishing

Prehistoric people hunted animals and gathered plants to survive. Historians believe that the most successful early people also fished. These people used pieces of bone, wood, or stone called gorges. The gorges were about 1 inch (2.5 centimeters) long. They were pointed at both ends. People covered the gorges with bait and attached a line to them. The gorge would stick in a fish's throat after the fish swallowed the bait. People then used the line to bring in the fish.

Freshwater fishing is one of North America's most popular sports.

Anglers can fish in freshwater sources such as streams, rivers, ponds, and lakes.

Other early accounts of fishing exist. Egyptian artwork from 2000 B.C. shows people fishing with rods, lines, and nets. Ancient Greek and Roman writings also have accounts of people fishing.

Fish were a major source of food for American Indians. They often used spears to pierce fish. This type of fishing is called spearfishing. Many American Indians still spearfish today.

In the early 1700s, people began to use rods with reels to fish. The reels were made of wooden spools. They allowed people to fish farther away from shore. People used the reels to quickly bring in or let out long lengths of line.

Today, most people fish with modern rods and reels. The sport also is called angling. Many North Americans angle both for recreation and for a source of food.

Types of Freshwater Fish

Anglers try to catch various types of freshwater fish. These fish live in water that contains very little or no salt. Freshwater includes streams, rivers, ponds, and lakes. Saltwater fish live in the world's seas and oceans. Salt water has a great deal of salt in it.

Some anglers try to catch small fish species such as white crappies and bluegill. Fish in the same species share certain physical features.

These small fish are called panfish. Panfish often live in shallow water close to shore.

Panfish eat insects, minnows, and worms. Minnows are small fish. Most minnows are about 2 inches (5 centimeters) long.

Anglers may try to catch large fish such as northern pike and muskellunge. These fish hunt small fish, frogs, and sometimes even ducklings. They have sharp, pointed teeth. They often live in deep areas of lakes near plants.

North American anglers also try to catch catfish. Catfish are bottom feeders. They eat small animals and plants at the bottom of a body of water. Catfish usually hunt at night. Catfish species include the bullhead, the flathead, the blue, and the channel.

Many anglers fish for trout and bass. Trout often live in cool, fast-running streams. These fish usually eat insects.

Bass often live in streams, rivers, and lakes. Bass eat insects, minnows, frogs, and crawfish. Crawfish are small freshwater animals that have hard outer shells.

Battered Fillets

Ingredients:

1 cup flour   Salt and
1 cup cornmeal   pepper
1 egg   Lemon wedges
1/2 cup milk
4 small fish fillets (boneless)
About 5 tablespoons oil

Equipment:

Small bowl   Metal spatula
Large plate   Paper towels
Medium bowl
Spoon, egg beater,
   or automatic mixer
Large frying pan

1. Combine 1 cup flour and 1 cup cornmeal in a small bowl and spread the mixture on a large plate.

2. Beat egg in medium bowl with spoon, egg beater, or mixer. Add 1/2 cup milk. Continue to beat until combined.

3. Dip each fish fillet in egg and milk mixture.

4. Press both sides of each fillet in flour and cornmeal mixture.

5. Add oil to frying pan until the bottom is covered about 1/4 inch (.6 centimeter) deep. Heat oil over medium-high heat until the oil becomes shiny and hot.

6. Sprinkle salt and pepper over the fillets.

7. Fry fillets about 5 minutes or until coating is golden brown. Turn fillets once with spatula. Repeat on the other side.

8. Drain on paper towels. Serve with lemon wedges.

Serves: 4   *Children should have adult supervision.*

CHAPTER 2

Equipment

Freshwater anglers need several pieces of equipment. They should have a rod, reel, and fishing line. Anglers also need hooks, bait, and lures. These wood, metal, or plastic objects are attached to hooks. Anglers use lures to attract fish. Anglers keep much of their small equipment in a tackle box.

Rods

Anglers can choose from a variety of rod types. Most modern rods are made of fiberglass or graphite. These materials are lightweight and strong.

Anglers use different rod lengths. Most freshwater anglers choose rods that are about 5 to 7 feet (1.5 to 2.1 meters) long. Anglers

---

Anglers can keep much of their small equipment in a tackle box.

use short rods for short casts. Long rods allow anglers to cast the line farther.

Most rods weigh between 2 and 4.5 pounds (.9 and 2 kilograms). Anglers who plan to catch large, heavy fish choose heavy rods. Anglers who plan to catch small fish choose lightweight rods.

Rods bend in a certain way. This movement is called action. Fast-action rods bend near the tip. Anglers usually put small bait and lures on fast-action rods. Slow-action rods bend closer to the rod's grip. Anglers often put heavy lures on slow-action rods. Beginning anglers often choose medium-action rods. These rods bend in the middle. They are suitable for a variety of bait and lures.

Some anglers who fish for panfish attach line to cane poles. These simple rods often have no reel. They usually are about 4 feet (1.2 meters) long. Beginning anglers also may use cane poles.

Reels

Reels allow anglers to control the line and the bait or lure attached to it. They also help anglers

Most anglers use rods that are between 5 and 7 feet (1.5 and 2.1 meters) long.

bring in hooked fish. The two basic types of freshwater reels are bait casting reels and spinning reels. Bait casting reels are heavier than spinning reels. They can handle a great deal of weight. Anglers usually use these reels to catch large fish. Spinning reels are light and easy to cast. Anglers usually use these reels to catch small fish.

Closed-face reels have a cover and a hole where the line comes out.

Spinning reels may be open-faced or closed-face. Open-faced reels do not have a cover. Closed-face reels have a plastic cover over them. The front of the cover has a hole where the line comes out. Open-faced reels allow anglers to cast greater distances than with closed-face reels. The line rubs against the hole on closed-face reels and causes a shorter cast. But closed-face reels provide anglers with more control over their cast than open-faced reels.

Modern reels have a switch or lever that puts the reel into freespool. Line is able to come off the reel during freespool. Anglers put the reel into freespool to cast. The weight of the bait or lure pulls line off the spool.

Reels also have an anti-reverse device. After a cast, anglers turn the reel handle. This action engages the anti-reverse device and locks the line in place.

Anglers adjust the reel's drag if they hook a fish. This device usually is located at the back of a reel behind the handle. A hooked fish often swims, jumps, or dives. The line could break if it stayed tight. But the fish could wrap the line around obstacles if the line was too loose. The drag on the reel should be set so that there is pressure on the line. But it also should allow a hooked fish to pull line off the reel.

Line

Anglers choose a line's strength based on the weight of the fish they plan to catch. Strength is measured by how many pounds the line can hold before it breaks. This measurement is called pound test. For example, 8-pound (3.6-kilogram) test can hold 8 pounds of pressure without breaking.

Anglers use monofilament or multifilament line. Most anglers use nylon monofilament line. This line has a single strand. It is strong and flexible. Multifilament line is made of braided threads of strong plastic called polyethylene. Multifilament line is five times stronger than monofilament line of the same thickness. It can hold larger fish than monofilament line. But multifilament line is more expensive.

Leaders, Sinkers, and Bobbers

Many anglers use leaders. These pieces of line usually are about 2 feet (.6 meter) long.

Anglers attach one end of a leader to the hook or lure. They attach the other end to a swivel at the end of the fishing line. This metal connecting piece has two small round holes.

Anglers sometimes put a snap on their leaders when they use lures. Snaps are small pieces of metal that look like safety pins. They allow anglers to easily change lures.

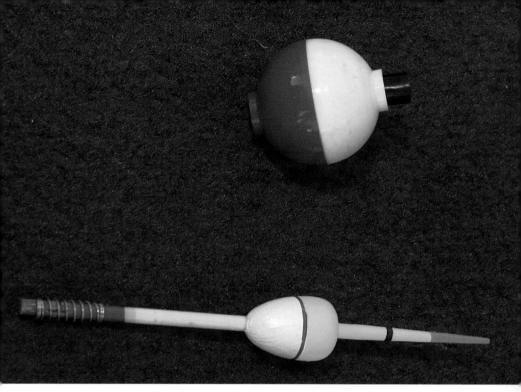

Bobbers keep bait at a certain water depth.

Sinkers are weights that keep bait or lures near the bottom of the water. Anglers may use small balls made of lead or other metals. In some states, anglers are encouraged to avoid using lead sinkers. These sinkers can be harmful to the environment. Sliding sinkers have a hole in the middle. A leader easily slides through these sinkers.

Anglers sometimes use bobbers with sinkers. These small floating objects attach to the line. They keep bait at a certain water depth. Anglers

Equipment

- Rods
- Fishing line
- Spinning reel
- Bait casting reel
- Bait
- Lures
- Leaders
- Snaps
- Sinkers
- Bobbers
- Hooks
- Net
- Clippers
- Forceps or pliers
- Map
- Hook sharpener
- Thermometer
- Water-resistant jacket
- Sunglasses
- Hat
- First aid kit
- Life jacket
- Depth finder

watch the bobber to help them know when a fish takes their bait. Most bobbers are brightly colored to help anglers see them.

Hooks

Anglers use a variety of fishhooks. Hooks are sized by number. Hooks that have high numbers are smaller than hooks with low numbers. Anglers choose hooks based on the size of fish they want to catch.

Many anglers use barbless hooks. Barbs are sharp points that extend from behind a fishhook's point. They help the hook stay in a fish's mouth. But barbed hooks are more difficult to remove from a fish's mouth than barbless hooks. Barbless hooks also cause less damage to fish than barbed hooks.

Clothing

Anglers wear clothes suitable for the weather. In warm weather, they may wear shorts and a short-sleeved shirt. But these anglers should bring warmer clothes in case the weather changes. In colder weather, anglers dress in layers. Anglers should have a water-resistant jacket in case of rain showers.

Anglers often wear life jackets. Unskilled swimmers and anglers who fish from boats must wear life jackets. Some anglers wear life jackets near streams and rivers with strong currents.

Other Gear

Anglers bring other gear on their fishing trips. They should have a net to help them handle hooked fish. They also need clippers to cut fishing line. Forceps or pliers can help anglers grip objects. They can use these items to remove a hook from a fish's mouth. Many anglers have a hook sharpener in their tackle boxes.

Anglers may bring a map of their fishing area. They can use the map if they become lost.

Many anglers use depth finders. These small electronic devices display the location of fish on a screen.

Anglers should bring other items. Anglers should always have a first aid kit. They should wear sunglasses and sunscreen to protect their

Anglers in boats always should wear life jackets.

eyes and skin from the sun. Many anglers wear
a hat to shade their face. Sunglasses and a hat
also can prevent fish hooks from getting into
anglers' eyes.

Some anglers carry a thermometer to
check the water's temperature. The ideal water
temperature varies according to the type of fish.
For example, panfish and catfish often live in
water between 75 and 80 degrees Fahrenheit
(24 and 27 degrees Celsius).

CHAPTER 3

Skills and Techniques

Beginning anglers should know the behaviors of different types of freshwater fish. These anglers also should learn what bait and lures to use to catch fish.

Finding Fish

Anglers can look for fish in a number of areas. Fish often lie near structures in the water. These objects can include rocks, docks, or submerged trees. Structures offer shady places for fish to hide. These objects also can create areas of slow-moving water called pocket water. Fish often rest in pocket water.

Anglers should learn about the different types of bait and lures before they fish.

Fish also gather near visible lines in the water called edges. Edges may form where fast-moving water meets calm water. They also may form where shallow water meets deep water. The lip of a dam or a line of weeds can form an edge. Edges often hold insects and plankton that fish eat. Plankton are tiny plants and animals.

Casting

Anglers start a cast with the pole in front of them. Anglers hold the rod in one hand with their palm facing down. They look where they want to cast. They also look around to make sure it is safe to cast.

Anglers follow several steps to cast. They first bend their wrist back and bring the rod behind their shoulder. They wait for the bait or lure to settle. They also make sure the line is not tangled.

Anglers then put the reel into freespool. Anglers who use bait casting reels place their index finger on the line to keep it from unreeling. Anglers who use spinning reels press a button on the reel's bottom. The anglers continue to look at the target as they quickly move the rod forward. They then lift their index finger or

Anglers can use a clock face to help them learn how to cast. They first bring the rod behind their shoulder and stop at 10 o' clock. They then start to bring their arm forward. Anglers release the button or lift their finger from the line at 1 o'clock. They stop the cast at 2 o'clock.

release the button as the leader flies past the rod's tip. This action lets the line out.

Bait and Lures

Anglers should know how to present live bait naturally. They place bait where fish would normally find it. For example, anglers place grasshoppers near the water's surface. They place worms near the bottom.

Anglers should know how to present different types of bait to fish.

Lures imitate the vibration, color, scent, or movement of food that a fish would eat. Spoons are made of shiny metal. These lures imitate small fish. Spinners have a thin blade that turns as anglers pull it through the water. Spinnerbaits and buzzbaits vibrate and shine.

Plugs imitate small fish, frogs, or mice. Some plugs float. Others sink to attract bottom feeders. Some plugs are crankbaits. Anglers reel in these lures underwater to attract fish.

Anglers also may use surface plugs. These lures float on the water's surface. Surface plugs sometimes are called topwaters.

Some anglers use jigs. These balls of lead are painted to look like an insect's head. Some jigs have strings of feathers or animal hair attached to them. Anglers place jigs near the bottom of a body of water. Some anglers add bait to jigs.

Freshwater Methods

Anglers in boats can use various methods to catch fish. They may allow the boat to drift with the wind and currents. They may troll. Anglers use a small motor to move the boat slowly through the water when they troll. They cast the bait or lure behind the boat. They then set the drag to keep the line tight. The movement of the bait or lure attracts fish.

From shore, anglers often cast out and reel in lures. Other shore anglers use bait. They cast and wait for fish to take the bait.

In streams and rivers, anglers often cast upstream. They then let the current carry the bait or lure downstream. Anglers reel in and start over when the bait or lure moves slightly past them.

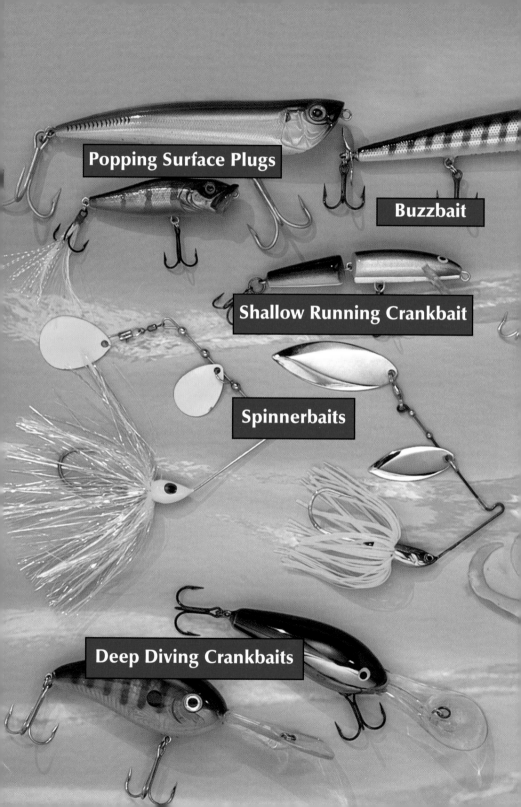

Popping Surface Plugs

Buzzbait

Shallow Running Crankbait

Spinnerbaits

Deep Diving Crankbaits

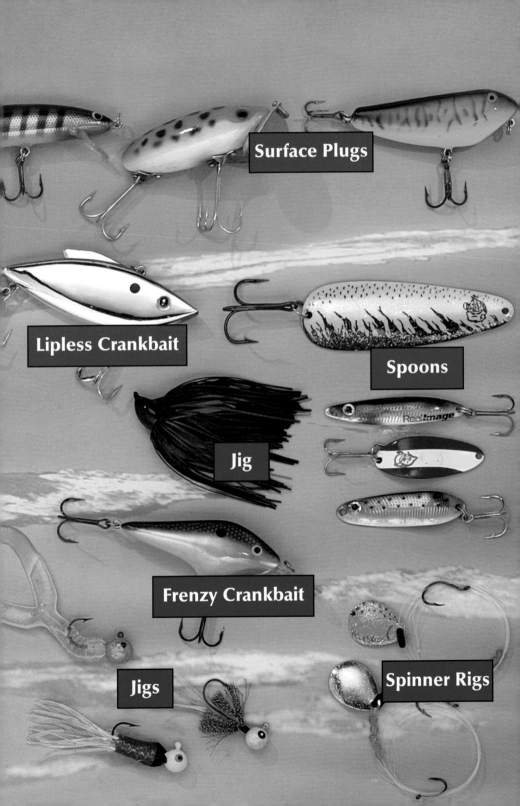

Surface Plugs

Lipless Crankbait

Spoons

Jig

Frenzy Crankbait

Jigs

Spinner Rigs

Conservation

Responsible anglers protect fish and their habitats. These are the natural places and conditions in which fish live. Anglers dispose of garbage and used fishing line properly. Fish and other wildlife may become entangled in fishing line or other items. Responsible anglers do not trample on plants or disturb wildlife.

Conservation Problems
Anglers who are not responsible can cause conservation problems. People sometimes take too many fish out of freshwater sources. This activity can change the balance of fish populations. For example, people may take too many large fish such as pike and muskellunge out of a lake. This action can cause the water

Anglers should release fish that they do not plan to eat.

Government agencies sometimes stock fish in water sources that have decreasing fish populations.

source to become overpopulated with panfish. Pike and muskellunge often eat panfish.

Pollution can damage freshwater sources. Farmers use fertilizer to make their crops grow. They use herbicides to kill weeds. These chemicals can enter water sources. Sewage and industrial wastes also can enter water supplies.

Polluted water causes many fish to die. Some fish can live in polluted waters. But poisons may build up in their bodies. These poisons can make them dangerous to eat.

Freshwater Improvements

Some laws help prevent further pollution of the nation's water sources. In 1972, the U.S. government passed the Clean Water Act. This law set guidelines for how industries should dispose of their wastes.

The U.S. Fish and Wildlife Service conserves, restores, and manages fish habitats in the United States. It also establishes wildlife refuges to protect fish, birds, and other animals. Hunting and fishing is limited or illegal in these areas.

The National Fish Hatchery System is part of the U.S. Fish and Wildlife Service. Members of this system raise fish in hatcheries. They then release the fish into water sources with low fish populations.

Many people form groups to improve fish habitats and increase fish populations. For example, Trout Unlimited and the Nature

All anglers need to follow government regulations.

Conservancy replace plants and gravel beds
that help fish spawn. Fish lay eggs when
they spawn.

Licenses and Regulations
North American anglers need to follow all
state or province regulations. These regulations

vary in the United States and Canada. Anglers of a certain age or older must buy fishing licenses. This age ranges from about 12 to 16. Anglers buy separate licenses when they fish away from their home state or province.

Limits regulate the number of fish a person can catch in one day. These limits vary according to the species and time of year.

People may catch most fish year-round. But some states and provinces have fishing seasons for certain fish species. For example, some provinces do not allow bass fishing until June. This regulation allows young fish to grow large enough to protect themselves. Some states do not allow people to fish in certain streams and rivers during spawning times.

CHAPTER 5

Safety

All anglers should follow safety guidelines. They should know the weather forecast and be prepared for severe weather. They should know basic first aid skills and be prepared for accidents.

Storms

Anglers pay attention to the weather forecast before they go fishing. They look for signs of approaching storms as they fish. Anglers may notice large, gray clouds or feel a sudden rush of cold air before storms. Many anglers have a radio to listen to weather forecasts.

Anglers in boats head for shore if a storm occurs. Anglers on shore stay away from tall trees, peaks, and other high objects. Lightning is more likely to strike these areas.

Safe anglers are aware of their surroundings when they cast.

Other Safety Guidelines

Anglers must handle fish carefully. They keep their hands away from the fish's mouth and spine. Some fish have sharp fins on their backs. Other fish such as perch have sharp gill covers. Fish breathe through gills. These openings are along the sides of a fish.

Anglers follow other safety guidelines. They stay away from litter that could cut or entangle them. Anglers in boats watch wave conditions. They learn where sandbars and other underwater objects are located.

Anglers need to be careful when they fish near streams and rivers. Rocks on riverbanks may be slippery. Streams and rivers may have powerful currents or underwater drop-offs. Water suddenly becomes deep at these places. Anglers should avoid entering a stream or river.

Anglers should know how to use the items in their first aid kits. These items usually include gloves, medicine tape,

Anglers on docks should make sure the structure is sturdy before they walk on it.

tweezers, scissors, and bandages. They also have gauze to cover wounds. Most kits have ointment to protect wounds from germs.

Safe anglers are prepared for unexpected situations. They help prevent accidents. These anglers make their fishing trips more enjoyable for themselves and others.

Rainbow Trout

Rainbow trout live throughout North America. They are common in northwestern areas of North America. These fish move from oceans to freshwater streams and rivers to spawn. Some rainbow trout live near Michigan in the Great Lakes area.

Description: Rainbow trout have silver skin covered with small black spots. A pink-orange band usually runs lengthwise along their sides. Their backs are blue-green to olive. Rainbow trout usually weigh about 2 pounds (.9 kilogram).

Habitat: cool, quickly flowing rivers and streams; some cool lakes

Food: insects, fish eggs, minnows, small fish

Bait and lures: nightcrawlers, minnows, salmon eggs, marshmallows, spinners, spoons, small minnow imitations, small plugs

Walleye

Walleye are common in the northern areas of North America. But anglers also can fish for them in some southern states.

Description: Walleye vary in color. They may be various shades of silver, yellow, yellow-red, or yellow-blue. They have small spots above their white undersides. Walleye have large eyes. They usually weigh about 3 to 10 pounds (1.4 to 4.5 kilograms).

Habitat: open areas in large lakes; cold, deep water near drop-offs and weeds in lakes

Food: minnows, small fish

Bait and lures: nightcrawlers, minnows, spinners, deep diving spoons, plugs

Northern Pike

Northern pike live throughout Canada and the northern United States.

Description: Northern pike are dark bronze. They are long and slim. Their tail and fins are red. Northern pike have rows of white and yellow spots along their sides. Scales cover their cheeks and the upper half of their gill covers. Northern pike have sharp teeth. They usually weigh about 4 pounds (1.8 kilograms).

Habitat: shallow, weedy areas; near structures

Food: other fish, frogs, ducklings

Bait and lures: large plugs, spinnerbaits, spoons

Flathead Catfish

Flathead catfish live in the central regions of the United States. They often are found in southern states such as Texas.

Description: Flathead catfish are pale yellow to light brown. They have small black or brown spots. Their belly is usually lighter than their sides and back. Their tail is slightly notched. Catfish have whiskerlike growths that extend from their lips. These growths are called barbels. The barbels help catfish feel their surroundings. They usually weigh about 10 to 20 pounds (4.5 to 9 kilograms).

Habitat: on the bottom of lakes and large rivers; near structures

Food: minnows, small fish, frogs

Bait and lures: chicken liver, cheese, pieces of hot dogs

Bluegill

Bluegill are common throughout North America. They are one of the most common types of panfish.

Description: Bluegill are bronze with about six dark bars on their sides. They have a large black spot on the edge of their gill covers. They also have a black spot at the edge of the dorsal fin. This fin is located on a fish's back near its tail. Bluegill have small mouths and oval-shaped bodies. They usually weigh about 1 pound (.5 kilogram).

Habitat: ponds, lakes, slow-moving rivers and streams with sandy bottoms; weedy areas, near tree roots and structures, shallow water close to shore

Food: insects, plants, fish eggs, small fish, snails, worms

Bait and lures: crickets, worms, caterpillars, grubs, grasshoppers, small spinners

Largemouth Bass

Largemouth bass live throughout North America. Two largemouth bass subspecies exist. The larger subspecies lives in Florida. The smaller subspecies lives in northern areas.

Description: Largemouth bass vary in color from green to dark gray. Most of these fish have a green back. Largemouth bass have a mouth that extends beyond the eye. They usually weigh about 10 pounds (4.5 kilograms).

Habitat: weedy, warm water in lakes and streams

Food: insects, minnows, frogs, small fish, snakes, turtles, ducklings, crawfish

Bait and lures: nightcrawlers, plugs, spinners, plastic worms, jigs

Words to Know

barb (BARB)—a sharp piece of metal that extends from behind a fishhook's point

drag (DRAG)—the device that places pressure on the line; anglers often adjust the reel's drag after they hook a fish.

edge (EJ)—a visible line where water changes or plants grow

freespool (FREE-spool)—a condition that occurs when line slips easily from the reel; anglers put their reel into freespool before they cast.

hatchery (HACH-er-ee)—a place where people allow fish eggs to hatch

plankton (PLANGK-tuhn)—tiny animals and plants that usually drift or float in oceans or lakes

troll (TROHL)—to fish by trailing a line with bait or lures from behind a slowly moving boat

To Learn More

Bailey, John. *The Young Fishing Enthusiast.* New York: DK Publishing, 1999.

Fitzgerald, Ron. *Essential Fishing for Teens.* Outdoor Life. New York: Children's Press, 2000.

Solomon, Dane. *Fishing: Have Fun, Be Smart.* Explore the Outdoors. New York: Rosen Publishing, 2000.

Sorenson, Eric L. *The Angler's Guide to Freshwater Fish of North America.* Stillwater, Minn.: Voyageur Press, 2000.

You also can read about freshwater fishing in magazines such as *In-Fisherman* and *Field & Stream.*

Useful Addresses

American Sportfishing Association
1033 North Fairfax Street
Suite 200
Alexandria, VA 22314

Canadian Wildlife Service
Environment Canada
Ottawa, ON K1A 0H3

U.S. Fish and Wildlife Service
4401 North Fairfax Drive
Arlington, VA 22203

Internet Sites

American Sportfishing Association
http://www.asafishing.org

GORP—Fishing
http://www.gorp.com/gorp/activity/fishing.htm

Trout Unlimited
http://www.tu.org

USAngler.com
http://www.usangler.com

U.S. Fish & Wildlife Service
http://www.fws.gov

Index